FIERCE
GIRLS

THIS BOOK
BELONGS TO:

Made with love by the team at

FiVE MiLE

Michelle, Rocco, Graham, Jacqui, Claire, Victoria, Sarah, Bridget, Tillie & Kate

Five Mile,
the publishing division
of Regency Media
www.fivemile.com.au

First published 2022
This paperback edition published 2023

Text copyright © Samantha Turnbull, 2022
Illustrations copyright © Kim Siew, 2022

Manufactured by Five Mile under licence from the Australian
Broadcasting Corporation. The ABC device is a trademark of
the Australian Broadcasting Corporation and is used under
licence by Five Mile
© Australian Broadcasting Corporation 2022.

A catalogue record for this book is available from the
National Library of Australia

Printed in China 5 4 3 2 1

FIERCE GIRLS

TEXT BY
Samantha Turnbull

ART BY
Kim Siew

FIVE MILE

Stand up, speak up, and never give up! These words fuelled my motivation and boosted my confidence whenever I was under pressure, wiped out or scared.

To be fierce means to be courageous, passionate, and focused. You need the courage to dream big and stay true to yourself. Passion empowers us to do the work, especially when we don't feel like it. Life is filled with distractions so being focused ensures we keep our eyes on the prize.

What does it take to achieve your goals? Clearly defined outcomes, a dream team of support we can rely on, and the discipline to always believe in yourself, despite any setbacks or obstacles, as these are stepping stones to success.

Never give up on your dreams because your dreams never give up on you.

Layne x

ABOUT THE PODCAST

Welcome to the *Fierce Girls* book!

We're so excited you get to now read some of the GREAT stories that we tell in the award-winning ABC podcast, *Fierce Girls*.

The podcast tells the stories of extraordinary Australian women including Julia Gillard, Celeste Barber, Layne Beachley, Evonne Goolagong-Cawley and Jackie French.

You hear stories about all sorts of women in the podcast – artists and aviators, adventurers and scientists, athletes and even spies!

Some of our favourites are the stories about Turia Pitt, Oodgeroo Noonuccal, Louise Sauvage, Cathy Freeman, Nancy Wake, Dr Catherine Hamlin ... oh, hang on ... we love ALL of them!

Each story you hear in the podcast is read to you by an extraordinary Australian woman.

We started the podcast after one of our fierce executive producers, Monique Bowley, said:

'Australian women are amazing! We should tell their stories to inspire kids across the world.'

So, we started telling stories, and 50 episodes later, we're STILL finding amazing girls and women to talk about.

Over the years, the podcast has had an uber-talented team of producers and audio engineers working on it. They all love this podcast as much as our loyal and fierce listeners. So a big shout out to the *Fierce* team: Monique Bowley, Justine Kelly, Kellie Riordan, Rachel Fountain, Judy Rapley, Tamar Cranswick, Sam Wicks, Alex Lollback, Laura McAuliffe, Rebecca Armstrong, Rashna Farrukh, Mark Don, Isabella Tropiano, David Le May and our awesome lead writer, Samantha Turnbull.

From the whole team, we hope you love this book! And when you're finished reading it, check out the podcast, free posters and colouring sheets at: abc.net.au/fiercegirls.

THE FIERCE GIRLS IN THIS BOOK:

PAGES 1–13

At school, Julia Gillard's least favourite subject was Home Economics. The teachers told her she'd need it one day, but Julia wasn't so sure. She had her mind firmly set on a career. First, she was a lawyer, then a politician, and later she became Australia's first female Prime Minister.

JULIA GILLARD

PAGES 14–25

Even as a young girl, Celeste Barber always had a funny story that would make everyone laugh out loud.

Celeste dreamed of starring in a TV comedy, and she went on to play a paramedic in a popular medical drama. When that series flatlined, she used Instagram to take the world by storm, one funny photo at a time.

CELESTE BARBER

PAGES 26–39

Surfer Layne Beachley grew up when girls were expected to sit on the beach and mind the boys' towels. Layne ignored that ridiculous rule and became the best female surfer in the world – seven times!

LAYNE BEACHLEY

PAGES 40–53

Evonne Goolagong-Cawley's first tennis racquet was a broomstick. Her second was a wooden paddle. It didn't hold her back. Evonne became the best tennis player in the world, winning 14 grand slams and Wimbledon twice.

EVONNE GOOLAGONG-CAWLEY

PAGES 54–62

Jackie French could read entire novels by the time she was three. But when she arrived at school, letters appeared back to front, and maths equations were gobbledegook. Jackie was confused, but it didn't stop her from reading, writing, or coming up with astonishingly creative tales. Jackie read everything in sight, and then decided to write her own stories.

JACKIE FRENCH

JULIA GILLARD

Labor

POLITICIAN

The koala fell out of Julia's arms, tumbling over the ship's railing and plummeting into the ocean.

'Nooo!' Julia screamed. 'Help him!'

But it was too late. The koala was lost in the ship's wake. An accidental burial at sea for the marsupial who would never make it to his native homeland.

Julia sobbed. Her mum, dad and big sister tried to console her, but it was hopeless.

'It was my koala,' Julia sniffled. 'He was brand new.'

Her dad patted her red hair and wiped the tears from her freckled cheeks.

'Julia, the koala was just a toy,' he said. 'You'll see real koalas soon.'

Julia Eileen Gillard was four years old and on a ship bound for Australia. She was born in Wales in the United Kingdom, known for its rolling green hills, castles, rugby and gloomy weather.

When Julia was a baby, she got sick with a chest infection that wouldn't budge. She had to keep warm so she wouldn't get sicker. She spent winter indoors, and in summer she was only allowed to dangle her feet in the pool while other kids splashed and swam. It was unfair and boring.

The family doctor advised them to move away. 'Somewhere sunny,' he said. 'With clean air.'

When the Gillards heard Australia wanted more people, they thought: 'Why not? It's hot!'

Julia's dad was especially keen for a fresh start. He was one of seven kids, and although he was super smart, he had to leave school when he was only 12. His family was poor and needed him to help put food on the table.

He worked in all sorts of jobs – shop assistant, coal inspector, policeman. But he always longed for school. And when he had two kids of his own, he made it his mission to make sure they never missed out.

'Gillard!' Julia's teacher yelled.

Fountains of soap suds poured out every crevice of the washing machine.

'Sorry, Miss,' Julia said. 'It must be broken.'

She was fibbing. Her friends giggled behind their hands. They deliberately filled the machine with an entire packet of detergent.

None of them understood why the girls at high school had to learn Home Economics – that's cooking, cleaning and sewing – while the boys got to build things with wood and metal.

'You'll need it one day,' the teachers reasoned. 'When you become a mum.'

But, at 16, Julia knew she never wanted to become a mum. It was just a feeling, and she was cool with it.

'I don't want to have kids,' she said. 'Not now, not ever. All I want is a good education and a good career.'

She had the good education sorted. Apart from the incident with the bubbling washing machine, Julia was a straight A student.

'ALL I WANT IS A GOOD EDUCATION AND A GOOD CAREER.'

She was shy, but when she joined the debating team, she came out of her shell. Debating wasn't just public speaking, it was arguing for something you believed in.

'Good afternoon, Chairperson, Adjudicator, audience and fellow debaters,' Julia said. 'Today, I will argue that women are just as capable of being leaders as men.'

When Julia was on stage with palm cards at the ready, she felt fierce. Her opponents would be shaking in their socks.

'I think I might become a teacher,' she thought. 'I love school, so it makes sense.'

But when she got the application forms for university, her best friend's mum said:

'You're such a good debater, maybe you should be a lawyer.'

A lawyer. It was just like professional debating. Standing up for people and fighting for what's right. That sounded like something Julia could do. She ticked the box. Law it would be.

'What do we want?'

'Better schools!'

'When do we want 'em?'

'Now!'

Julia didn't wait to become a lawyer to start standing up for people and fighting for what she believed was right.

She bought herself some no-nonsense, lace-up army boots and led uni-student marches, demanding better and fairer education for all.

It felt exhilarating. Making a stand. Calling for change.

Julia thought back to her parents talking over the dinner table about a political group called the Australian Labor Party. They told her the party fought for workers' rights and top education for everyone, no matter how much money they had or where they were from.

A light bulb flicked on in Julia's brain: 'I need to join the Labor Party!'

So, she signed up.

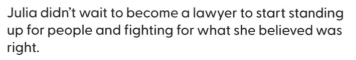

All the important Labor bigwigs noticed Julia, and it wasn't just because she was a woman in a room full of men in business suits. She walked with her head held high. She was a confident, successful young lawyer. But she had her eyes on a new career.

Julia didn't just want to be a member of the Labor Party, she wanted to represent them as a proper politician.

She went to meeting after meeting, shaking hands, rubbing shoulders. She was trying to convince the men in suits that she belonged in the most important building in Australia, Parliament House.

'Come on,' she said. 'Let me have a go. Let the public vote.'

Yet Labor wouldn't do it.

Maybe it was because Julia was young. Maybe it was because she didn't have enough experience. Maybe certain people just didn't like her. But Julia never thought it was because she was a woman.

'I know I can do it, you know I can do it. So let me try!' Julia said.

Finally, after years of Julia hustling, the Labor party realised she wasn't going to give up.

'You've shown us how determined you are,' they said. 'We'll give you a chance.'

They probably wished they had done it earlier, because almost three-quarters of the people in Julia's neighbourhood voted for her. She was in!

Julia got lost a lot in Parliament House. It had more than 4,000 rooms inside. But when Old Parliament House was built it didn't even have a women's toilet.

Women weren't even allowed to vote when Australia's first government was formed. Once they could vote, it took 41 years for the first women politicians to get a spot in Parliament.

When Julia took her seat in the House of Representatives – that's one of two main rooms in Parliament where laws get made – she was sitting alongside 14 other newly elected women. 11 of them were from her own party.

'IT IS A CAUSE FOR CELEBRATION AND WILL INSPIRE US TO ENSURE THAT MANY MORE WOMEN FOLLOW US INTO THIS PARLIAMENT.'

She didn't like to make a fuss about being female, but she had to admit it was an epic feeling to see women's faces dotted among the rows and rows of men.

'It is a cause for celebration,' Julia said in her very first speech. 'And will inspire us to ensure that many more women follow us into this Parliament.'

But just because she was there, it didn't mean she was in control. Julia spent nine long years in Parliament in the Opposition – that means your political party isn't the one calling the shots.

It was kind of like sitting in a building where half the people were powerful, and the other half wanted to be. Julia was on the side that wanted to be.

But Julia's frustration turned to hope when an election was called – that's when the people of Australia get to vote for who should be running things in Parliament.

The leader of the Labor Party was a man named Kevin Rudd.

'Julia, I want you to run alongside me,' he said. 'As my second-in-charge.'

If Labor won the election, Kevin would be Prime Minister and Julia would be Deputy Prime Minister. They were on the verge of making history because no woman had ever been Deputy Prime Minister of Australia before.

Julia never thought about the fact she was a woman because it wasn't a big deal to her. She just wanted the job.

'I'll do it,' she said.

Julia pulled back her shoulders. Deputy Prime Minister. It sounded good. And she knew she was up to the task.

'And the results are in,' the newsreader said. 'It's a clear swing ...'

Julia was being filmed for live TV when she heard.

The votes had been counted.

A smile spread across Julia's face. Labor won! Easily!

'Shhh!' Julia quietened down her supporters. Everyone around her was cheering so loudly she couldn't hear a thing.

She stayed calm for the cameras, said her thankyous and goodbyes, then jumped in a car with a chauffeur so she could head home to celebrate properly.

They were waiting at a red light when Julia noticed something out of the corner of her eye.

It was two teenage girls in the next lane. They wound their window down and their arms were flailing wildly.

'What is it?' Julia called out.

The girls were screaming, but not in a distressed way. They were ecstatic.

'It's her!' they said. 'It's you! Julia! Julia Gillard!'

Congratulations!'

After keeping composed all night, Julia felt a rush of excitement. There was no denying that moment was anything but awesome.

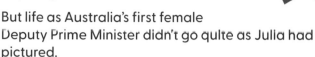

But life as Australia's first female Deputy Prime Minister didn't go quite as Julia had pictured.

Some of her Labor mates didn't like Kevin Rudd. Whispers and he-said-she-said stories swirled through the corridors of Parliament House.

Julia feared such trouble could destroy her party, so she took a deep breath and knocked on the Prime Minister's door.

'Kevin, I'd like to challenge you for the leadership,' she said. 'We'll let the party vote. If they choose you, you stay as Prime Minister. If they choose me, I take over.'

Kevin shook Julia's hand. But, after realising he wouldn't get enough votes, he bowed out of the race.

It was a strange way for it to happen. There was no fanfare, no party, no teenage girls waving to her from a car window. But, Julia Eileen Gillard had just become Australia's first female Prime Minister.

She was almost blinded by the cameras flashing when she was ready to make the formal announcement. The media were desperate to know what happened behind closed doors.

'Julia, how do you feel?'

'Julia, why did you do it?'

'Julia, are you a traitor?'

Julia was careful not to smile too much. She wanted people to know that it was a serious occasion. No-one thought you should be proud of pushing a workmate out of their job and then taking their place.

'A good government was losing its way,' she said.

Julia said it over and over again. It was a rehearsed line, deliberately vague.

Julia vowed to let the Australian people decide themselves whether she should stay. They would get to keep her or boot her out in the next election. Until then, she would do her best as the new boss of the country.

The contest was tight. So tight, that after the voting finished, it took 17 days for Julia to find out for sure that she had won.

As her Labor party mates hugged and hooted around her, Julia let out a massive sigh.

'Phew! That was too close.'

Julia made it through by the skin of her teeth.

Once she knew she would be staying on as Prime Minister, she rolled up her sleeves and set to work.

'Now, let's get on with the job,' she said.

But a curious thing happened. No-one seemed to focus on the job Julia was doing. They were more worried about what she was wearing.

On her first day, journalists obsessed over Julia's coat. One writer described it as looking like a cheap motel bedspread.

Julia attended important meeting after important meeting ... and instead of wondering what happened, the world would criticise her clothes.
If it wasn't her suits, it was her make-up, or her body, or her red hair. Everyone had something to say about the red hair.

Julia laughed it off.

'It's a good day for red heads,' she said in her first interview as Prime Minister. The journalist was also ginger-haired.

'IT'S A GOOD DAY FOR RED HEADS!'

When Julia visited schools and saw a red-headed kid, she was always sure to say: 'Hey, nice hair!'

No-one cared what the male politicians wore, or about the size of their butts, or if their hair was dyed, or if they had any hair at all.

That one thing Julia had never thought was a big deal – being a woman – was suddenly a big deal for everyone around her.

She tried to ignore the nastiness, but it got harder and harder to shake it off.

Her opponents teased her for having no children. One cattle industry boss compared her to a useless old cow during a speech at a fancy dinner.

A famous radio announcer said she should be thrown into the sea, like her old toy koala. Other haters carried signs that called her a witch and vile names that are too rude to repeat.

All of it hurt Julia. All of it made her angry. But she held it inside.

Until ...

Her nemesis, the leader of the Opposition, dared to accuse Julia and her party of treating women unfairly.

Julia stood tall behind her microphone in Parliament, and unleashed her most passionate speech of all time.

Julia pointed her finger, listing the horrid comments and insults she and other Australian women had endured.

'We are entitled to a better standard than this,' she ended, before taking her seat, unaware that her rant was about to go viral.

The speech was watched and shared by millions of people across the globe.

Julia Eileen Gillard spent three years and three days as Prime Minister of Australia.

She believed her biggest achievements were helping make life easier for people with disabilities, protecting the environment, improving schools and forming solid friendships with other countries.

She never wanted to make a big deal about being a woman. But in her final speech as the nation's leader, she had a message for the girls of Australia: Don't ever give up.

'I am absolutely confident it will be easier for the next woman, and the woman after that, and the woman after that. And, I'm proud of that.'

CELESTE BARBER

COMEDIAN

'Can you look at the sun without blinking for five minutes?'

The religion teacher waited for an answer.

Celeste scrunched up her nose and narrowed her eyes into teeny-tiny slits. Then, she blinked.

'Nope,' she said. 'I can't do that, Miss.'

Celeste was only eight, but she was pretty sure it was dangerous to stare directly at a searing ball of gas for any length of time.

Her teacher replied: 'Well, if you can't look at the sun for five minutes without blinking, you don't love Jesus.'

It was possibly the most ridiculous and random thing anyone had ever said to Celeste. And, maybe, it was the moment she realised you couldn't believe everything people told you ... even very important people.

But, it was also a funny story that made everyone laugh. And making everyone laugh was what Celeste Elizabeth Dominica Barber did best.

'Hey, guys! Did you see *Friends* last night?' Celeste asked her schoolmates. 'Could Chandler BE any more hilarious?'

Celeste's favourite television show was *Friends*. She memorised every laugh-out-loud line and recited them at school the next day.

'Oh, oh – want me to sing *Smelly Cat*?' Celeste said. 'Smelly caaaaat, smelllllly cat, what are they feeding youuuuu?'

Celeste cracked up. But her friends weren't laughing. In fact, they weren't even looking at her.

'Oh no,' Celeste sighed. 'Not you too.'

A couple of mean girls had decided they didn't like Celeste. She was never quite sure why, but assumed it was because she was loud. She was the type of kid who was often described as 'over-the-top,' 'full-on' or 'out-there'. Celeste, mostly, took it as a compliment.

But the mean girls didn't give compliments. They were on an anti-Celeste quest and instructed all the other students to ignore her. So, like brainless minions, they did.

Until, one morning when Celeste stepped off the school bus, a boy rushed up to her frothing with excitement.

'You're going to get bashed at lunch time,' he said. 'The other girls say so.'

When the lunch bell rang, Celeste slowly made her way to the playground. A crowd of blood-thirsty spectators gathered in waiting.

'Fight, fight, fight,' they chanted.

One of the mean girls lunged at Celeste.

'Ah!' Celeste stumbled back like a clumsy giraffe. And then she ran. She ran, and she ran, all the way to the safest place she knew ... the library.

Celeste's heart was pounding. Her hands were shaking. She tried to calm herself down by writing something funny. She scrawled her name over and over again:

Celeste Barber.

Celeste Barber.

Celeste Barber.

Celeste Barber is the best, chuck out the rest!

CELESTE BARBER IS THE BEST, CHUCK OUT THE REST!

Celeste was determined not to let the other kids break her, no matter how hard they tried. And they tried hard. Very hard.

The anti-Celeste quest went on for a whole entire year. 365 long days of being ignored by everyone at school except the teachers.

Her drama teacher helped to lift her spirits (and didn't make her stare at the sun).

'It's good to be different,' she told Celeste. 'Be loud and proud.'

'Challenge accepted,' Celeste said.

She immersed herself in the drama room, dancing, singing, acting and telling jokes.

'CHALLENGE ACCEPTED!'

'One day, I'll be on a TV show just like *Friends*,' Celeste thought. 'And all of this will be a distant memory.'

Take one!

'Doctor, the patient is suffering from ventricular fibrillation!' Celeste said. 'We need a defibrillator, stat!'

Celeste had made it. She grew up and became an actor. Her first big role was playing a TV paramedic on the popular medical drama series, *All Saints*.

'YOU'RE BETTER SUITED TO COMEDY.'

But as Celeste's stardom rose, the series flatlined.

'Don't worry,' her friends said. 'You're better suited to comedy, anyway.'

Celeste was also a mum and, in between changing nappies and auditioning for acting roles, she downloaded a new social media app called Instagram.

'It's like all the best bits of a magazine,' she said. 'Endless photos of fancy people, fancy places, fancy food, fancy clothes – I'm hooked!'

But after hours of scrolling on her smartphone, Celeste noticed a definite difference between what she saw in the glossy pages of her favourite magazines and on the Instagram grid.

'No-one poses on top of a skyscraper in a ballgown at sunrise with a wind machine,' Celeste thought as she flipped through her magazines. 'Everyone knows the stuff on these pages is a fantasy.'

But the people on Instagram seemed to be tricking their followers. They were pretending their lives were a fantastical picture-perfect fashion shoot ALL.THE.TIME.

'Look at that mum picking up the kids from school on her luxury yacht,' Celeste scoffed. 'Look at that dad and his 17-ingredient green smoothie he makes every day for breakfast, right before his 28-step skincare regime and his 76 chin-ups.'

Celeste didn't buy it. Neither did her sister, Olivia.

'I wonder what I would look like trying to do these rich people things,' Celeste said.

Olivia's brain sparked like a light bulb.

'Take some photos and see,' she said. 'It'll be funny.'

That was all Celeste needed to hear. She was good at funny.

'Challenge accepted,' she said.

Celeste asked herself two questions before every photo shoot:

1) What will I look like doing that?

2) Will it make people laugh?

'TAKE SOME PHOTOS AND SEE. IT'LL BE FUNNY.'

If the answers were 1) funny and 2) yes, Celeste struck a pose.

Her first muse was a super-flexible yogi model posing with her legs stretched up against a ballet bar.

Celeste copied, but her back was hunched and her bent legs were hanging over a railing in her lounge room.

She took a photo and captioned it: 'I'm starting something, #challengeaccepted.'

Then, Celeste recreated socialite Paris Hilton's windswept hair with her husband's air compressor.

Then, she copied reality TV star Kylie Jenner's super-sized pout by smearing lipstick all over her face.

Then, she tried to mimic model Gisele Bündchen's head throw back, and almost put her neck out in the process.

The laughing emojis trickled in underneath Celeste's photos.

But it wasn't until she sprawled out in her undies, on a big pile of dirt, that the world really sat up and noticed Celeste Barber.

#CHALLENGE ACCEPTED!

'LOOK, FELLAS, THINGS ARE ABOUT TO GET WEIRD!'

Dressed in high heels, fish-net stockings and a trench coat, Celeste marched down the street to her local BMX track. A couple of teenage boys were there.

'Look, fellas, things are about to get weird,' Celeste said. 'I'm going to take some inappropriate photos, so ...'

The boys skedaddled.

Celeste set up her camera and draped herself over a dusty mound. She recreated the most absurd shot starring one of the biggest influencers on social media, Kim Kardashian.

Celeste captioned the pic: 'Don't you hate it when you fall over on a dirt pile and your husband demands a photo shoot? I do.'

Celeste's followers grew from a few thousand to tens of thousands, streaming in every few minutes. Even the celebrities she copied left comments of approval:

'Celeste, can I share this photo?'

'Celeste, you forgot to tag me!'

'Celeste, I've got another photo you can do!'

The phone rang.

'CELESTE, YOU FORGOT TO TAG ME!'

'Celeste!' her acting agent said. 'I'm being inundated with media requests. Everyone wants to interview you about this 'hashtag challenge accepted' thing you're doing. What is it anyway?'

Celeste scratched her head. She wasn't really sure.

The media bombarded Celeste with questions.

'Are you making fun of these people?' a reporter asked.

'It's not so much the people I'm making fun of, it's the culture,' Celeste said. 'And myself ... I'm making fun of myself.'

Another reporter asked: 'Celeste, are you being trolled for being overweight?'

'Yeah, some people are telling me I need to lose weight, but I don't care,' Celeste said. 'I think I look good.'

'Celeste, how does it feel to be a feminist icon and body-positive role model?' another reporter asked.

Celeste shrugged. 'Am I?'

The truth was, Celeste didn't start copying celebrity Instagram snaps to make any smart statement about body image. If her photos made people more comfortable with the way they looked, it was just a happy side effect.

'I don't compare my body with the bodies of people I parody,' Celeste said. 'I just want to be funny.'

'I just want to be funny.'

'I just want to be funny.'

'I just want to be funny.'

'I JUST WANT TO BE FUNNY.'

Celeste was funny, but she was also Instafamous. And as her followers grew and grew into the millions and millions, big businesses wanted a piece of Celeste's pie, too.

Requests streamed into Celeste's inbox:

'Please plug our detox tea.'

'Our weight-loss pills could really help you slim down.'

'Your followers might like to try our meal replacement shakes.'

Celeste had a one-word answer for all of them: NO.

'I don't promote any products that make women think they need to look a certain way to feel a certain way,' she said. 'And, while we're at it, why do we spend so much time talking about how we should or shouldn't look anyway? Let's talk more about how we feel.'

Meanwhile, Celeste was feeling a tad peeved with everyone describing her as an Instagram star. She was so much more than that. She was an actor and a comedian.

Celeste never thought of Instagram as a proper job, just a platform for sharing stuff. But, it was a platform that came in handy in a moment Celeste never could have predicted.

'It's Joy,' Celeste's mother-in-law said down the phone line. 'The town is burning and no-one is here!'

Joy was living in the middle of a bushfire. Celeste could hear the panic in her voice.

'I'll help you,' Celeste said. 'I don't know how, but I'll think of something.'

'THIS IS TERRIFYING, PLEASE HELP ANY WAY YOU CAN.'

Celeste wished she could grab a hose and put out the fires herself, but she lived too far away from the disaster zone. So, she did the next best thing she could think of. Celeste picked up her phone and started recording a message for her Instagram followers.

'Australia is burning,' Celeste said. 'This is terrifying, please help any way you can.'

Celeste posted a link for people to donate to the NSW Rural Fire Service. She set a goal of $30,000.

She didn't have any expectations. Maybe people would ignore her. It wasn't a funny post, after all.

So, she posted and waited.

'Wait ... what?' Celeste couldn't believe her eyes.

Everyone – from celebrities to everyday people – shared and donated, donated and shared.

Within hours, they raised more than $100,000. By nightfall, it was half a million.

'This is AMAZING!' Celeste squealed. 'Thank you so, so much!'

More than one million people from more than 75 countries chipped in.

By the time Celeste's campaign ended, she raised more than $50 million. That was enough for 50 luxury apartments, 50 solid gold toilets or 50 first-class, round-the-world trips.

But Celeste wasn't interested in what the uber-rich would do with the cash. All she knew was what she wanted to do: Help people in a crisis, like Joy, to realise that they weren't being ignored. They weren't alone.

Challenge accepted. Challenge conquered.

Celeste Barber was way more than an Instagram star. She was a hero. And she had the last laugh.

CHALLENGE ACCEPTED!

LAYNE BEACHLEY

SURFER

Boom!

His words hit her with more force than any wave that had ever knocked her from a surfboard.

Boom!

She could see his lips moving, but her mind was filling with the same white noise that follows a massive wipe-out.

Boom!

He gently placed his hand on her shoulder.

'Do you understand, Layne?' he asked.

She slowly nodded. She may have been only eight years old, but she knew what her dad meant when he said:
'We love you ... but we got you from somewhere else.'

Boom.

Just like that, Layne Beachley found out she was adopted.

Perhaps she should have noticed earlier that the puzzle pieces didn't quite fit together. Her mum, or adoptive mum as it turned out, was part-Japanese.

Her adoptive dad had fair skin and towered over them.

Layne looked completely different. She was tanned with bleached blonde hair and sparkling blue eyes. She was also tiny. Everyone nicknamed her 'Gidget' after a famous, teeny weeny, surfer-girl character from a 1950s novel.

But, at that moment, Layne felt more like Alice in Wonderland, shrinking to the size of a bug and being swallowed by the couch. It would have been a perfectly normal reaction for little Layne to hide like a bug in a cocoon.

It wasn't the first time she'd been hit by a tidal wave surge of shock. The woman she called 'Mum,' the one who adopted her, died when Layne was only six.

Boom.

If there was anything that was going to crush Layne, that would've been it. But Layne wouldn't let herself be crushed. And she didn't hide in a cocoon.

Layne told herself that if her birth mother didn't love her enough to keep her, the rest of the world would adore her instead.

In fact, the very same day Layne found out she was adopted, she promised herself she'd become the best in the world at something ... anything ... she just wasn't sure exactly what.

Layne was one of the sporty kids at school. She was good at soccer, tennis and cricket. If it took a bit of strength, coordination and speed, Layne could do it.

But it was the beach that was Layne's special place. Her earliest memory was being plonked on the sand with her bare, baby butt on show, squealing with joy as the waves rolled in.

She started learning to surf when she was four. Her board was a 'foamie' – made from foam – soft and safe, perfect for beginners.

Layne stood up and caught small swells as the ferries pulled in. But before long she wanted more: A real board, real waves, real adrenaline.

She upgraded to a fibreglass model and paddled into a break called North Steyne. It was a gutsy move. North Steyne was known for being one of the most territorial surf spots in Sydney. The waves belonged to the salty old locals. If you dropped in on them, you'd be minced meat.

It wasn't just the 'locals only' rule that was dangerous. Layne stuck out like a proper sore thumb in her bikini. In the early 80s, surfing wasn't exactly a female thing. A girl's job was minding boys' towels on the beach. So, when Layne dared to join the blokey line-up in the water, they thought she was asking for trouble.

LAYNE STUCK OUT LIKE A PROPER SORE THUMB.

'Grrr!'

The guys growled at Layne like menacing dogs. They tugged at her leg rope, and deliberately splashed her in the face.

One man yelled: 'You're a girl – get out of the water!'

As quick as a wink, tween Layne yelled back: 'What are you doing out here, then?'

Layne came up with a name for guys like those meanies. She called them 'dream thieves', and she refused to let them steal from her.

As impossible as it seemed, Layne knew she'd found her thing: Surfing. She vowed to become the best in the world.

It was time. Layne was 14 and about to enter her first proper contest. She was the only girl in a sea full of boys.

Layne dug her arms into the water, paddling furiously onto wave after wave, determined to prove herself. She jumped to her feet, turned with all her might and flicked off, ready for the next set. And then …

Boom.

Reality hit. Again. Layne came dead last.

Layne wondered if she really had what it took to be the world's best. Were the dream thieves right?

'Nup,' she thought.

Layne was no towel-minder. She dusted the sand off her board and paddled out again.

LAYNE WAS NO TOWEL-MINDER.

She even thanked the boys who beat her, because they'd taught her a lesson.

She obviously needed to practise, and so that's what she did. Paddled and practised. Practised and paddled.

Until ...

Boom!

Layne started beating the boys. A sick heat at a local boardriders' contest turned the tide.

Layne scribbled in her diary that night:

I got a filthy left, did the biggest backhand cover-up, then grabbed my rail and came out of the barrel and tried to turn and my front foot slipped off. I was spewing! But it was the filthiest backhand barrel I've ever had!

Fresh out of high school, Layne was living the dream ... almost. She was surfing in contests across the globe, but she could barely afford her plane tickets.

Layne had to work three jobs to raise the cash she needed to surf. She was a shop assistant, barmaid and pizza delivery driver. She worked until 2am, then got up to surf at sunrise.

Most of the men had sponsors like surfwear companies paying for their trips. Plus, they easily earned more than 10 times the prize money of the women.

Meanwhile, Layne and her surfer-girl buddies would hitchhike from beach to beach and sleep inside their board bags because they couldn't afford hotels.

But nothing was going to stop Layne Beachley. After everything she'd been through, scraping coins together was water off a pelican's back.

Even as a pro, Layne was always trying to improve.

'I surf like a crab,' she told her coach. 'How do I get better?'

Layne put a finless board on top of her bed and practised jumping to her feet in one smooth motion. She did it over and over again, every morning and every night until she had it mastered.

All the while, dream thieves tried to bring Layne down.

'It's not going to happen,' they said.

'You can't afford to do that.'

'You're not smart enough.'

'You're not talented enough.'

'You're not valuable enough.'

And, all the while, Layne told herself:

'I can.'

'I will.'

'I am.'

'I CAN, I WILL, I AM!'

There was no better fuel than the negativity of those dream thieves.

After eight years of missing out on the world title by a handful of points, Layne was on track to make it happen. She'd already won a wave of contests and she could smell victory on the horizon.

Layne was in France, more than 15,000 kilometres from Australia. Yet Layne had never felt more at home.

The sea had always been the place Layne could go to escape and, in that moment, she felt like there was no-one else in the world out there but her.

PADDLE, STAND, SHRED.

She caught every wave like clockwork. Paddle, stand, shred. Paddle, stand, shred.

She turned her board so sharply spray whipped up behind her from the force.

As the waves closed out, she'd flick off, ready to go again.

Layne was calm. Layne was cool. Layne was ready.

When the siren sounded and the crowd on the beach erupted, Layne almost didn't notice.

'Nouveau champion du monde de surf!' the announcer declared.

She cupped her ear, straining to listen.

'Huh? I don't speak French, what are they saying?'

The announcer was declaring Layne Beachley as the new world champion of surfing.

Boom!

It finally hit her.

Layne had pictured the moment a million times, but it didn't happen how she'd imagined. There was no tense final showdown. Layne had just won a basic first-round heat, but her build-up of points across the tour had pushed her into an unbeatable position.

She splashed her hands in the water with delight.

'Finally,' she laughed. 'I did it!'

It wasn't a surprise. Layne had worked harder than anyone. She deserved the world title.

But there was one surprise to come.

Layne received a phone call, practically moments after she propped her trophy up on her mantelpiece.

'Hello, Layne?'

It was a woman named Maggie.

'I'm your mum,' she said.

Boom.

It was another moment Layne had pictured a million times, but, again, it didn't happen how she'd imagined.

Instead of feeling happy, Layne felt weird. Maggie had given her away when she was a baby, and that was a hard thing to understand.

Layne agreed to stay in contact with her birth mother, but she didn't get too close. She didn't want to get hurt.

Besides, she had more world titles to win.

Layne won the crown again the following year. And again. And again. And again. But it was the sixth that brought the most pressure.

Layne was in Hawaii, floating among some of the heaviest waves in the world. She was hanging out the back, but she wasn't feeling her usual oneness with the ocean.

Self-doubt crept in. The voices of dream thieves thumped in Layne's head.

'You can't do it,' they told her. 'Your time is up.'

Boom!

Six world titles in a row would make Layne the most successful surfer of all time, boy or girl, man or woman. She wondered if she should just settle for five and stop being greedy. Maybe it was time to give someone else a chance.

'You can't do it,' Layne told herself. 'You can't break the record.'

She was panicking. She was floundering. She was losing it.

Boom!

A familiar sound managed to snap Layne out of it. It wasn't crashing waves or squawking seagulls. It was one of her favourite rap songs booming over the speakers from the shore. The lyrics told her to go for it. It was her one shot.

The ocean swelled. That familiar wall of green water began to form right in front of Layne.

Her opponent was too far out to catch it. It was now or never.

Layne told herself again: 'You CAN do it. Go!'

She focussed and paddled as the water pushed her forward.

She jumped to her feet in one perfectly smooth motion.

She crouched as the wave curled around her like a cuddle. She was inside the tube ... it was every surfer's dream.

Time stood still as the water wrapped around Layne. She was in a never-ending cave, with green as far as the eye could see.

She could've stayed there forever, but if she wanted to win, she needed to find the exit. Layne looked up, but there was no light at the end of the tunnel. Just water. And more water.

'I'm not going to make it out,' she thought. 'It's over.'

The crowd thought the same. Layne had been inside the barrel for so long that people were turning away. They assumed she'd fallen off, swallowed by the sea.

Then ... Boom!

A hole appeared.

Layne surged ahead towards the open end of the tube and catapulted out.

The crowd was stunned. Layne was too.

'Ten!' the judges roared.

Layne raised her arms in disbelief.

A perfect score. And her sixth back-to-back world title.

Layne had done what no surfer had done before.

She was a record-breaker. The best ever.

A few years later, Layne won her seventh crown and retired from the professional tour.

But her work wasn't done. Layne knew there were plenty of dream thieves in the world, so she decided to become a dream-maker.

Layne dedicated herself to helping other women conquer the surfing world. She didn't want them to have to hitchhike and sleep in their board bags like she did.

She even started her own women's contest, paying more prize money than any other event on the tour, and launching the careers of today's world champions.

Now, thanks to Layne, the best women surfers are winning cheques with the same number of zeroes as the men. They don't need to hitchhike and sleep in their board bags anymore.

And, when a girl paddles out into the line-up anywhere from Australia to France to Hawaii ... she knows she belongs there.

EVONNE GOOLAGONG-CAWLEY

TENNIS PLAYER

'Kids, quick, hide! It might be the welfare man!'

Evonne Goolagong's mum knew how to scare her and her seven brothers and sisters.

Whenever there was an unexpected knock on the door, she told her kids to take cover in case they got stolen.

They were Aboriginal – Wiradjuri – and they had heard about other Koori kids disappearing.

The government sent scary men out in big black cars to snatch brown-skinned children from their families. They took them far away to try to make them live like white people.

Luckily, it never happened to Evonne. But it did make her nervous around powerful men – people like police officers and other official-looking types.

It also made her stick close to her family. They were the only Indigenous people they knew of in Barellan, their tiny home town.

But on weekends they packed up the car to visit the rest of their mob in communities bounded by the three great rivers, the Lachlan, Murrumbidgee and the Murray.

'Got your ball, Evonne?' her dad asked as he started up the engine.

Some kids had blankies. Some kids had dummies. Some kids had teddies they carried everywhere.

Evonne had a tennis ball. She found it under a car seat, greasy and scuffed. She didn't even know what it was but she always held onto it, squeezing it without realising she was strengthening her wrists.

'No fair, Evonne,' her cousins said. 'You're too strong!'

The other kids couldn't get her out in cricket. No-one could beat her in any sport. She was a natural-born runner, swimmer, hitter, catcher. But more importantly, in Evonne's mind, sport was fun. Sport made her smile.

SPORT MADE HER SMILE.

So, when the Goolagongs pulled into their driveway and saw some men building what looked like a rectangular sports field right near their house, Evonne's heart skipped a beat.

'What is it?' she whispered.

Her mum laughed. 'It's a tennis court, silly.'

Evonne had never seen a game of tennis. She peeked through the fence watching as players hit a white ball back and forth.

'That looks easy enough,' she thought.

Evonne copied, hitting her ball against the brick practice wall. She didn't have a racquet, so she used a broomstick.

'Here you go, love,' her dad said. 'Try this.'

It was a wooden paddle made from an apple crate. It was a bit of a cross between a tennis racquet and a cricket bat, but Evonne sure could whack with it.

Twenty-five. Thwack.

Twenty-six. Thwack.

Twenty-seven. Thwack.

Evonne counted how many times she could hit the ball in a row.

Twenty-eight.

Thwack.

Evonne used a twig to etch her scores in the red dusty earth, then started again from zero.

One. Thwack.

Two. Thwack.

Her powerful thwacks caught the eye of the tennis court owner. He invited Evonne inside to play a proper game with her older sister, Barbara.

Evonne was only seven, three years younger than you were supposed to be to join the club. But Evonne and 10-year-old Barbara easily won a doubles game against some older kids.

'How'd it feel to win?' everyone asked.

Evonne shrugged and smiled. 'It was just fun to play.'

Grown-ups started to whisper about Evonne.

'She's one to watch,' they said.

'She could be the next big thing.'

'Tennis star in the making, that girl.'

Evonne ignored them, burying her head in a magazine called *Princess*. A story inside distracted her from the adults' conversation. It was a fairytale:

Once upon a time, there was a girl who loved to play tennis.

She was poor, but she practised and practised.

She became so good, she went to Wimbledon.

She won, and lived happily ever after.

'Wimbledon, hey,' Evonne said. 'Never heard of it, but it sounds like the place for me.'

Evonne's mum and dad drove her, Barbara and their brother Larry to tennis tournaments all over the bush.

They won almost every match. They even won against men and women three and four times their ages. Evonne beat everyone from teachers to doctors to policemen.

'Guess I don't need to be nervous around these official-looking types after all,' she thought.

But she still wanted to stay close to her family. So, it was a tough choice to move to the big smoke when a tennis coach offered to train her there full-time. Evonne was still a kid, and would have to change schools and make new friends.

'You'll be right, love,' her mum said. 'You don't have to hide anymore.'

The whole of Barellan helped Evonne off to Sydney by raising money for her trip. A seamstress even made her a crisp, white, tennis dress to replace the one her mum had sewn from an old bed sheet.

'We're proud of you, Evonne,' the townspeople said at the airport.

Evonne kissed her mum, dad, brothers and sisters, and turned to board the plane.

She took one last look at them before she walked through the door. Everyone was sobbing. Evonne's throat wobbled, but she held her tears in.

But when Evonne arrived in the city, she cried into her pillow every night because she missed her mob so much.

She was torn between her dream and her home.

'We've come to watch the little Aboriginal girl,' strangers said.

Evonne's matches drew huge audiences. Lots of people hadn't seen an Aboriginal tennis player before.

Reporters called her 'dusky' and 'tawny' and 'piccaninny' – a rude and racist word sometimes used in the olden days to describe dark-skinned children.

But Evonne wasn't offended when people told her they were fascinated by her colour. She just grew tired of always talking about it.

'What's it like to be an Aborigine?' people asked.

'Can you speak some Wiradjuri for us?'

'Do you know how to throw a boomerang?'

Evonne was proud to be Aboriginal, but she wanted the world to focus on her tennis.

She cut out the newspaper headlines she actually liked:

'Wimbledon here I come!'

'Evonne moves closer to a place in Wimbledon squad.'

'The strong young legs of Evonne, our bright, new star!'

She pasted them in a scrapbook.

'These ones are right,' she said. 'I will be off to Wimbledon soon.'

Wimbledon was the world's most prestigious tennis tournament. Evonne didn't know that when she read *Princess* magazine, but she sure did know it when she got there. It was a Grand Slam in England, the land of tea, scones and posh people.

Evonne giggled when she walked onto Centre Court and the band broke out in *Waltzing Matilda* instead of some fancy-pants orchestral piece.

'Once a jolly swagman, camped by a billabong,' the singer crooned.

The Aussie theme was laid on thick, because it wasn't just Evonne in the final. She was up against the best woman tennis player in the world – Evonne's idol and fellow Australian – Margaret Court.

But Evonne wasn't intimidated when she met Margaret's eyes across the net.

Margaret looked serious and steely, but Evonne couldn't stop grinning. She thought she might explode from joy and excitement.

The English newspapers nicknamed Evonne 'Sunshine Supergirl', and that's exactly how she felt.

'You've got nothing to lose,' she repeated to herself. 'Nothing to lose, nothing to lose, just have fun, just have fun. Nothing to lose, just ... have ... fun.'

Evonne bounced from foot to foot on the baseline, eagerly waiting to play.

Margaret had the first serve.

Thwack.

Evonne hit it back easily.

'GO SUNSHINE SUPERGIRL!'

The crowd roared. 'Go Sunshine Supergirl!'

They were on Evonne's side. They wanted the cheerful underdog to win, not the well-known champion who already had the title.

Evonne smiled and hit. Backhand, forehand, drop shot, slice, top spin, flat, side, volley. She pulled out all the stops, effortlessly floating across the court.

Margaret was nervous. She was fumbling.

Evonne was relaxed. She was enjoying herself.

'Game, Miss Goolagong,' the umpire said over the loudspeaker. 'She leads the first set, four-games-to-love.'

Evonne was making it look easy, until Margaret fought back.

'Game Mrs Court, three-games-to-four,' said the umpire.

Margaret was clawing within reach, but Evonne wasn't fazed. It only made the match more fun.

Thwack!

'Game, first set, Miss Goolagong.'

Evonne had never had so much fun in her life. Winning a set in the Wimbledon final was surreal.

Winning a second set was everything she'd ever dreamed of.

'Game, set, championship, Miss Goolagong,' the umpire said. 'Thank you linesman, thank you ball boys.'

It was all over in 63 minutes. Evonne defeated Margaret 6–4, 6–1.

She ran to the nets and shook Margaret's hand.

'Thank you,' she said. 'That was fun!'

Margaret hid her disappointment: 'Congratulations, Evonne.'

Everyone in the stands rose to their feet, clapping and hooting.

Ball boys in green and purple shirts formed a guard of honour for the presentation ceremony.

Evonne walked through in a daze, too overwhelmed to properly take everything in.

She curtseyed to British Princess, Alexandra, who was about to hand Evonne the biggest prize in women's tennis – a shiny silver platter known as the Venus Rosewater dish.

'And the Wimbledon champion of 1971 is Evonne Goolagong!'

Evonne's smile out-sparkled the trophy in her hands. She raised it into the air, turning in a circle so everyone could see.

'Hooray, Evonne!' the crowd cheered.

'Hooray, Australia!'

Evonne didn't know it at the time, but her family was crowded around the television in their lounge room at Barellan. They were celebrating with fish and chips.

'She did it!' they screamed, jumping up and down, hugging and crying. 'You beaut!'

Evonne missed them. She wished they were at Wimbledon. She wanted to go home.

She flew back to Australia as quick as she could.

Barellan's population swelled to more than five times its size, as people from far and wide crammed onto the footpaths to catch a glimpse of the new champion.

20 trucks were turned into floats, with every sports club in the community joining a parade through the streets, led by Evonne and her family.

'Welcome home, Evonne!' the crowd called out.

'We love you, Evonne Goolagong!'

'You're our hero, Sunshine Supergirl!'

Evonne's cheeks were stained with happy tears.

The rest of Australia might have thought Evonne belonged to them, but her hometown knew she would always belong to the Barellan War Memorial Tennis Club.

Evonne soaked in the celebrations, knowing she couldn't stay. She wasn't finished on the world stage yet.

Some people didn't understand that Evonne played tennis for fun more than anything else. She didn't always win, but she didn't particularly mind.

'Aren't you upset?' her coach asked.

'No,' Evonne shrugged. 'It was a fun game.'

Sometimes, when she appeared to have a lapse in concentration, reporters would say she'd gone 'walkabout'. It was a white man's word sometimes used to describe Aboriginal people who strayed off track.

Evonne didn't let it bother her. She took tennis seriously, but it was still just a game. There were other parts of life to live, too.

She got married and changed her name to Evonne Goolagong-Cawley. She also had a baby girl.

'Evonne Goolagong's career is over,' the newspapers said.

'Evonne Goolagong is a has-been.'

'No more Sunshine Supergirl.'

Her coach even quit because he didn't think marriage and tennis stardom mixed.

Evonne wondered if she should quit, too. But something deep inside told her to keep going. As long as she thought tennis was still fun, it was still worth it.

Nine years after her first Wimbledon final win, Evonne was back on Centre Court.

Her opponent was American superstar, Chris Evert-Lloyd.

'Quiet please,' the umpire said over the loudspeaker.

Black storm clouds hung overhead. It was a fitting scene for Evonne's new serious approach. She was determined to win this time. She still wanted to have fun, but she was fully focussed.

Thwack.

Thwack.

Thwack.

It worked. The first set was quick.

'Game,' the umpire called. 'First set Mrs Cawley, six-games-to-one.'

Evonne was one game up in the second set when the clouds burst.

'Run for cover!' everyone yelled.

Evonne and Chris sat in the change rooms, waiting out the storm.

'Come on,' Evonne grumbled. 'Rain, rain go away.'

They had to wait for a whole hour before they were allowed back on the court.

The disruption rattled Evonne.

She was up three-love, when Chris unleashed a flurry of furious winners.

'Game, Mrs Lloyd,' the umpire said. 'She leads the second set, four-games-to-three.'

Chris hit the lead, bringing the score to 6–5. If she won the next game, the second set was hers.

'I'm not going to let that happen,' Evonne said under her breath.

Evonne brought the score to 6–6 and took the set to a tie breaker.

The spectators were on the edges of their seats.

Evonne and Chris whacked the ball over and over, in one of the longest rallies Wimbledon had ever seen.

One. Thwack.

Two. Thwack.

Three. Thwack.

Luckily, Evonne was used to counting her hits, and felt completely comfortable racking up the tally.

Thirty. Thwack.

Thirty-one.

The ball didn't return. The rally had finished. Evonne won.

'Game, set, championship, Mrs Cawley,' the umpire said. 'Thank you linesman, thank you ball boys.'

Evonne raised her arm in the air. She had finally done it. If the reporters didn't want to call her Sunshine Supergirl anymore, they could call her Sunshine Supermum instead.

It was the fairytale Evonne had read in *Princess* magazine, but it wasn't make-believe:

Once upon a time, there was a girl who loved to play tennis.

She was poor, but she practised and practised.

She became so good, she went to Wimbledon.

Evonne Goolagong-Cawley's happily ever after came when she moved home to Australia.

She is known as one of the all-time greats of tennis.

Today, Evonne is in charge of a foundation to help Indigenous kids like her achieve their dreams. Lots of the boys and girls have no idea who Evonne is, but she shows them the old piece of wood that she used as her first makeshift tennis racquet.

'See this,' she says. 'It shows that you can start anywhere, with anything. All you need is a dream ... and to have fun.'

JACKIE FRENCH

AUTHOR

'Jackie! Dinner time!'

Jackie French couldn't hear her grandmother. She was too busy playing in her imaginary land.

She had a friend there called Little Tending Girl – 'tending' was short for 'pretending', because Jackie knew her friend was imaginary.

'Come on, Little Tending Girl,' Jackie said. 'Let's go chat to the sparrows.'

At dinner time, her grandmother always opened the window and set a place at the table for birds to flutter in and take a nibble. Jackie liked how they shared their space with wildlife.

Jackie loved to tell stories to the animals, birds and Little Tending Girl, but they were mostly based on books she had already read.

And Jackie read everything she could.

She read the newspaper, she read the phone book – a giant, old-fashioned book that had millions of names and phone numbers in it.

Then, she went to the library and read everything in the children's section. And then, when she'd done that, she read almost all the books that were meant for adults.

By the time she was three, Jackie could read novels, thanks to her grandmother's teaching.

But when Jackie started school, something a little strange happened. She couldn't read spelling lists on the blackboard. Words and letters would appear jumbled and back-to-front. And maths equations were gobbledegook.

But, she wasn't bothered. Jackie sensed she was very clever.

No-one else her age was reading Socrates – he was a famous philosopher Jackie liked to have imaginary conversations with. And no-one else finished a whole textbook in an hour or two.

Her super-speed reading meant she was often left bored in class while everyone else played catch-up. She'd stare out the window and daydream.

But, mostly, Jackie's teachers could see she had a special talent for storytelling.

On a Sunday afternoon, when Jackie was six years old, she ran out of books to read.

'I know what I'll do,' Jackie said. 'I'll write my own book!'

The words spilled messily from pen to paper.

'Tresses and the Unghostly Ghost – good title,' Jackie said. 'This is more fun than reading!'

The story was about a horse who tried to escape from a ghost. He fell down a cliff and died. Then, the horse became a ghost and was reunited with his dead master.

'It's dark,' Jackie thought to herself. 'And, yet, a happy ending!'

She took the book to school.

'Jackie French, this is remarkable,' the headmistress said. 'I'm going to print copies for every single student.'

Jackie puffed out her chest proudly, but something about it didn't feel quite … original.

Her story was a mish-mash of other books she'd read. A cross between *Black Beauty* and something by Enid Blyton.

She shared her worries with Little Tending Girl.

'I wonder if I could write a story that was completely mine,' Jackie said. 'My own special magic.'

Little Tending Girl replied: 'You should speak to my big sister. Her name is Maria.'

Suddenly, a new imaginary friend appeared. Maria.

'Don't be afraid,' Maria said. 'All you need to do is send your mind off with the wind. That's where stories come from.'

And, from that moment, Jackie's stories didn't come from the pages of other books. They came completely from her mind. Made from her own special magic.

Every afternoon at school, if everyone had behaved, the teacher would let Jackie tell them a story.

'There once lived a girl called Mary ...'

Jackie's classmates were enthralled.

'She lived in a cave, at the bottom of a volcano.'

They hung on every word.

'But one day, there was a tsunami ...'

'Thank you, Jackie, that's enough for today,' the teacher said. 'We look forward to hearing the rest tomorrow.'

Jackie lingered at the teacher's desk.

'Miss, do you think I could become a famous writer?' she asked. 'Like Charlotte Brontë or Socrates?'

The teacher looked down on Jackie with kind eyes and a sympathetic smile.

'I'm afraid not in Australia,' she said. 'Writers don't earn enough money to make a living here.'

It wasn't the last time an adult said those words to Jackie. So, eventually, she believed them.

But Jackie could never give up writing all together.

She wrote when she was happy.

She wrote when she was sad.

She wrote when she was scared.

But, mostly, she wrote because it was fun ... more fun than anything.

If she couldn't be a paid author, she decided she'd live like the characters in one of her favourite books – *The Magic Pudding*.

'I'll have a huge garden ... no, a food forest!' Jackie said. 'And we'll live in harmony with all of the animals ... and every night we'll feast on what we've grown ... and we'll eat as much pudding as we like!'

When Jackie grew up, she bought her magic-pudding dream. Her own slice of bushland, complete with swimming holes, sunbaking skinks, fig trees and friendly frogs.

There was just a slight problem.

Jackie didn't have any money left over for anything else. The feasts she'd always dreamt of had to be foraged.

Jackie's tummy growled, and she had to get ... creative.

She singed the fur from moths and fried them up for visitors and drank echidna milk.

And there was no grand homestead.

Instead, Jackie lived in a tin shed that she shared with a wallaby named Fred, a black snake named Gladys and a wombat named Smudge.

There were no lights, no TV, not even a fridge to keep the echidna milk cold.

'I think I need some money, Smudge,' Jackie said. 'Let's see if I can write a children's book … and convince someone to pay me for it.'

Jackie dusted off her old typewriter. It was covered in wombat poo.

'Hmmmm, the 'e' key is broken,' she said. 'Never mind. I'm sure whoever reads it can make sense of the words without the letter 'e'.'

Jackie typed and read. Read and typed. Until, she'd written a collection of short stories called *Rain Stones*, inspired by her beloved bushland.

'Done!' she declared.

She gathered up the pages and did her best to wipe away the remnants of Smudge's droppings.

'Never mind,' Jackie said. 'I'm sure whoever reads it won't mind a little smear of wombat poo.'

The publisher was surprised by Jackie's letter. She laughed at the dirt and the missing letters.

'I like it. The stories are good. And this Jackie French person has certainly captured our attention,' she said.

'Dear Ms French.

We are pleased to inform you that we would like to publish your book.

Kind regards,

Angus & Robertson.'

Jackie shared the news with Smudge.

'Well there you go,' she said. 'Maybe you can make money from writing, after all.'

Her *Rain Stones* book was shortlisted for one of the most prestigious literary prizes in the country – the Children's Book Council of Australia awards.

'MAYBE YOU CAN MAKE MONEY FROM WRITING, AFTER ALL.'

And, now, publishers can't get enough of Jackie French's manuscripts – wombat poo and all.

Jackie has written more than 200 books for children, adults, and everyone in between.

She writes about growing food, being kind to the planet, the bush, history, natural disasters ... and wombats.

Jackie's bestselling book still makes her smile – *Diary of a Wombat*. And it also makes her money.

Jackie has moved out of the tin shed and into a house made from stone, where she eats as much pudding as she likes.

She's packed away her broken typewriter and bought a computer. And she's discovered there is a label for the trouble she has always had with words and numbers – dyslexia.

But Jackie isn't bothered. She still senses she is very clever.

'Computers can write neatly and computers can correct your spelling,' Jackie says.

'But, computers cannot daydream. Only you can send your mind off with the wind. That's where stories come from.'

'COMPUTERS CANNOT DAYDREAM.'

FIERCE GIRLS